Spaces In Time

Spaces In Time

Prose and Poetry
by
Larkin Stentz

© 2012 by Larkin Stentz
All rights reserved. First edition 2012.

No part of this book may be reproduced or transmitted in any form or by any means, graphic, electronic, or mechanical, including photocopying, recording, taping, or by any information storage retrieval system, without the permission, in writing, from the publisher. This book is a work of fiction. Names and characters are of the author's imagination or are used fictitiously. Any resemblance to an actual person, living or dead, is entirely coincidental.

Mystic Lights Publishing
West 4th Avenue RPO
PO Box 19173
Vancouver, B.C. Canada
www.mysticlightspublishing.com

ISBN: 978-0-9784986-3-4

Cover and Book Design by Julius Kiskis/Kiskis Designs
kiskisdesigns@comcast.net
Cover illustration by Rhonda Grudenic

20 19 18 17 16 15 14 13 12   1 2 3 4 5

Contents

Preface vii
Deeper Rhythms 2002 1
Night Bird 1982 2
Who 1982 3
Time and Space 1982 4
Light Song 6
Harmony 7
Moment of Silence 2011 8
Flower 2011 9
Moment in Time 1976 10
Pleasures of the Soul 1980 11
Petals Unfolding 2002 12
Hellebore 2002 13
Naked Standing 2002 14
You Give Me Pause 2002 15
Stretching 2002 16
Don't Tell The Sun 2002 17
Striving 1980 18

Contents

Come Watch 2005 19
Listen to the Wind 2002 20
Embracing 2002 21
Love Lying 2002 22
Lingering 2002 23
The Mound 2002 24
Words 1975 25
Walk With Me 2002 26
Like Elephants 1995 28
Six Months 1995 30
Limbo Land 1995 31
Owl Call 1980 32
New Sailors 1982 34
Reflection 1985 35

Cover Image: Higher Path, oil on panel, 30"x21"
by Rhonda Grudenic at grudenicburke@yahoo.com

Larkin Stentz * P.O. Box 1229 • Long Beach, WA 98631
larkinstentz@mac.com

Preface

What was thought at first to be a Christmas gift of poems for a few friends has emerged as a poetic journey of moments over 40 years.

Grateful am I for my friends who love me, wrinkles and all. To inspire me to put this collection together has offered the opportunity to reflect on the layers of my tapestry. As words in a poem by Michele Easton - Cortright expresses - "We weave our lives in many colors..." so within this collection are many colors within the tapestry of my life. I see them as glimpses of my emersion in the layers of life's mystery. Some glide over moments, seeing the textures on the surface. Some come from deeply swimming in the waters of my emotions. Still others are observations from that spiritual realm from which we receive guidance. And others, who knows?

Some poems seem to have come with one line to impart. Like "personality bound being unfolds..." is one such line that has a story all its own.

It is my hope that one of these will give you pause, to consider the colors in your tapestry.

In Joy -
Larkin
02/2012

Deeper Rhythms

There are deeper
rhythms that we must
dance to
other than the calendar of events
our culture prescribes.

Night Bird

The night bird calls
> deep,
from a meadow within.

Few hear
or pay any heed.

Snow and ice
> cover the ground,
The seed hears
> sleeps
> grows
> grows ready for spring.

Look
inside...
what seeds have you planted,
> forgotten?
Listen
> the night bird calls
> Will your spring bear fruit?
> Or have you forgotten
>> to tend your seed?

Who Among Us

Who among us speaks even half a truth?

Is the earth not in crisis?
Is childbirth not a crises - mother and child both
    dancing on the edge.
    Earth mother is in labor now
    We are the star child,
    From our mother we have received
and to her we must give,
Then, then, then from this giving
We shall have everlasting peace.

Time and Space

That pregnant place
In Time and Space
Where past and future memory
meet in a vision of one
throughout eternity.

A time no place
has yet been found
To call home for this vision
to be ground.

In the air, sea, fire and soil
lie the memory
all beings - one.

The time is now
the place within
the seed grows
of one vision to begin.

Comes forth the seed
from within
the knowing soul

Breaking through the ground
Of the personality bound
being - unfolds.

Hearing the call
in an ancient tongue
it speaks...

"Live the souls desire,
create the music
dance the dance
form the vision
of the oneness all aspire."

Light Song

Light Song On A Bird's Wing

Harmony

*H*armony predisposes differences.

Moment of Silence

In a moment of silence

A million suns are born,

Which one are you?

Flower

When all about is chaos,

A flower blooms -

Be that flower

A Moment in Time

A moment in time as midnight passes quietly on busy streets.
Somber reflections on the now and then of yesterday.
Becoming whole with moments in the universe is being.
Frustration is a configuration for maintaining the past,
eating leftovers day after day until they are gone -
then to cook a configuration again.
Without sadness there is no drama, no actors but especially no roles or scripts to read -
after all, how many comedies do you know?
Laughter is love, God and oblivious harmony.
I'm so scared of being well!

Pleasures of the Soul

Passion lies beneath my soft exterior friend,
I am a warrior for the pleasures of the soul.
Fantasies strip away our cloths, embracing, intertwining,
waters disintegrating the differences.
Wakefulness creeps over our recent history,
we see a new world of differences now.
The warrior sleeps,
exhausted in another attempt to satisfy the pleasure
of the soul.

Petals Unfolding in the Light

Petals unfolding in the light
    With memories of seasons past
Warm springs that faded too soon
    Hot summers that lingered too long
Brilliant fall colors
    That seemed to last forever
Winter dreams of all things beautiful.

Petals unfolding in the light
    of our love
Bring up memories, some deep and dark
    Others high and bright.
Staying present with our light
    Looking at all the remembered seasons
        That arise
And throughout the journey
    Our light will shine
As we embrace the day
    And hold in the night
Unfolding new petals
    of delight.

Oh Hellebore

Oh Hellebore
        Gift of love and so much more...
Through snowy nights
        Your countenance bears
So at morning light
        You blossom bright and fare...

As winter's darkness wanes
        Your strength unfolds a beauty with wings...

Other colors now too appear
        A primrose, a violet, a forsythia fare
But none can compare
        To the hellebore
        A gift from my amore
        That lights my heart
        And so much more.

While Naked Standing

While naked standing at my door
Having showered and nothing more
Hung a single ripe strawberry
From the basket you made with such merry.
Gently pulling it from the vine
It came easily to be mine
Slowly melting ripe juices on my tongue
My mouth seemed to swell with sweetness when I was done.
With the strawberry made merry from the rich soil of your garden floor
I stood delighted and naked at my door
And nothing more.

You Give Me the Pause

You give me the pause to connect
You give me the rhyme to reason
You give me truth for the telling
You give me light for the shadows
You give me mountains for the valleys
You give me the ocean for the rivers
You give me the rain for the clouds
You give me the spirit for the breath
You give me the melody for the music

You give me to me
        and in all of this
You give me love
        and I am nourished.

Stretching

Stretching, flowers move
>to the light
Soft bells of blossoms
>ring in the night
Subtle fragrances
>whisper soft graces
And the fairies sing
>of sweet Carol
>gardener of delight.

Don't Tell the Sun Not to Shine...

Don't tell the sun not to shine
    Because you're having trouble with your mind...
Don't tell the river not to run
    Because your life has only just begun...
Don't tell the forest not to grow
    When the hair on your head is all you have to show...
Don't tell the moon not to rise
    Because you have dark glasses over your eyes
Don't tell the wind not to blow
    Because you're growing way to slow
Don't tell the flowers not to emerge
    When it's anger in your heart that you need to purge
Don't tell me not to love
    Because it's your fear you can't rise above

The Sun Shines
The River Flows
The Forest Grows
The Moon will rise
And the Wind will blow
And the flowers will show
That love will always grow
Because love was their beginning
And
Love
Is
Neverending.

Striving

Striving ceases, the seed of truth unfolds
>the difference
>the oneness
both, - hands for the pleasure of the soul.

Come Watch the Crows Gather

Come watch the crows gather
From my perch among the clouds
We'll lie and spoon to warm another
As we whisper dreams we journeyed upon

Come watch the crows gather
As morning light grows its embers
Lighting sky and earth with flowing fingers
Lying still in warm embrace
Our wanting soothed by night's loving grace.

Come and watch the crows gather
With salmon and azure sky
To and fro their cedar spire
They bring on the day with a cacophonous choir

Come and watch the crows gather
As the light of a new day dawns.

Listen To the Wind

Listen to the wind in the trees
I will sing to you with the breeze
Soft melodies of dancing hands
      Loving bodies lying twined on the land

The plants listen as we sing
      our love song
Laughter and delight
      find comfort in our light

Listen to the wind in the trees
I will sing to you in the breeze
Soft melodies for dancing hands
      and loving bodies lying on the land.

Embracing

Embracing as we lay
Your head on my chest
My fur cradles your face
Your fingers comb
the trees of my forest

Breathing we blend
And there is no beginning
nor end...

I Love Lying With You

I love lying with you in the morning
    Soft light bathing your skin
The fit of our bodies - then
    A shift, a move finds
    Oh yes
That spot that fits so nicely.

I love lying with you in the garden
    Gazing at nature's bounty
    Smelling the rich soil
    Hearing the birds and the breeze
Watching your hair catch a wind
And ride up to my face laughing
Holding, our dancing fingers
    Touching, tracing the hills and valleys
    To a rhythm all their own and...
The garden laughs with delight.
I love lying with you on the floor
    Your head on my shoulder
    Arms intertwined, hands holding
    And we laughing.
Sometimes standing and holding
    Is lying together
In the kitchen, swaying, embracing
    Turning around and stirring
    Nibbling, kissing and stirring
    Our insides and breakfast, lunch and dinner
    Oh, what a seasoning.
I love lying with you
    in the afterglow of our loving
As the embers of millions of our cells
    Sigh,
    And we breath and become breath...
I love lying with you...

Larkin Stentz

Lingering and listening

The morning waves crashing
Alders budding, rustling in the wind
Early Robin announces, awake, awake
And the clear memory of your visit still lingers

Like a fragrance with vision
You saw the TV on
      there was no sound
And Pshta, a glance
not to be found.

I watched as your loving gaze
      Rolled over memories
      Our love making
      Our laughter
      The light through the windows

Your presence lingered
      As I drifted into sleep.
To wake and remember
You visited last night,
      how nice.....

(Pshta is my feline friend)

The Mound

I like the mound just above
    the folds of your yoni
I imagined cupping your mound today
    while working in the garden.
I cupped you,
    You moaned, and your waters began...

With my palm I slowly did small circles
    slowly parting your lips
    exploring your tender folds
You moaned, and your waters flowed

You moaned your pleasure
    as your head leaned back
    and your eyes closed.

Words

I send out words like carrier pigeons,
Hoping for their return,
Acknowledgement of my ownership.

Come Walk With Me

You beckoned and said
> Come walk with me
> And I cried

I walked with you
> On the beach
> Side by side

You holding my arm
> Lovingly looking into my eyes
> You said
> Come walk with me
> And I cried

We walked and walked
> Erupting from deep within
> Sobs emerged
> Cleansing old times that had been

And you said
> Come walk with me
> And I cried.

Mile after mile
> Flowing, old pain came out

I cried, a part of me is dying
> You said, yes, it is letting go
> And I cried

Mile after mile
> Memory upon memory
> Waves releasing and joining the sea

And you said come walk with me
> And I cried

Later you beckoned,
> Come walk with me

Now we walked arm in arm seeing
Trees, iris and water hyacinth blending
And the power within grew again.
We walked and with each step
> Loving wisdom now claimed

The spaces where tears had cleansed
You beckoned
> Walk with me
> And I did
> And we grew.

Like Elephants

Like Elephants with their tusks
    gently caressing the bones
    of their departed companion

I sway, my head, back and forth
    Looking, remembering, feeling your
    Preciousness

I sense your eyes behind, alongside, with,
    part of my eyes -
Seeing your's looking at me
    with the love only your eyes can speak.
My - our eyes touch our things,
    hold them as the gifts they are...

Watching in my mind the elephants
    tender remembrances
    drawn from bone.

I can understand now
        those that hold onto ashes
        there is history there -
A tome of knowledge
        in the dust of those fibers.

I feel heavy and substantial
        As an elephant
Weight like waves
        back and forth
Passing from foot to foot
        a long tear stream
        leading from the eyes
The tusk lifting, nuzzling, turning over
        the bones
Sipping last fragrant fragments
        of loving character
Oh - were I an elephant
        how I would honor your bones
I am elephant - I honor your bones.

Six Months

So tear full yesterday
The ocean of emotion
Dissolving all my senses

No one time or place now
A handful of unmolded clay
All the feelings
        All the tears
        All the fears
        All the rage
        All the love
              Melding
      Molting
Re modeling my soul
Into what, whom, when

Change is merging with my path
And coaxing movement
Toward some where new
Life
with and without
You

Limbo Land

Limbo land
Not old
Not young
    Ha Ha Middle aged
Not lesbian
Not gay
Widowed, alone.

The birds come every morning for feed
Trees stretch in the morning sun
Kale flowers nod yes, no, maybe

Everything sets - still
A picture which once captured a moment in time
Struggles in my mind to come alive again

No, that would truly hurt I think
Then, going on would have to start all over again.

Becalmed in this middle zone, limbo land
Not old
Not young
Widowed - alone

Maybe if I blow on the sails, whew, whew, whew, whew....

And The Owl Called His Name

We had known each other for over ten years. Our time together covered a spectrum of events and emotions from the mundane to the unbelievable.

Yet the events of our last week together were like the final coalescing of pieces of a puzzle which only came together after ten years.

Kidney failure was the diagnosis. The lost appetite, the limp, the constant sleeping were all symptoms. The clarity in the eyes remained. The looks that said so much and never failed to make their impression.

In a remote, quiet place the call came. To me it was just the calling of an owl, but to him... a calling which he answered - immediately. The answering sound came from a deep place within him. He followed the call, walking into the night. God knows how he walked, he had been bed ridden for ten days. I followed.

An old path was found, even in the dark. Funny, years earlier when we had first found this path I had remarked how it would be a good place to "crossover." And now here he was beginning his final journey.

After what seemed endless stopping and starting a pause came in our journey. Tired and not really thinking the time had come, I picked him up and carried him back.

Not two minutes had we returned when the call came again and again he answered and again he headed for the door. I surrendered to his timing now.

During the next twenty hours or so we walked, stopped, napped, walked, stopped, etc... We must have said farewell a hundred times. His eyes stayed clear and he spoke of letting go and how wonderful our friendship had been.

Sleep finally came over me and when I awoke he had crossed over. The tree where he is buried blooms with periwinkle year round now.

In the evening of the day he crossed over I was roused from sleep by screeching and the pounding of wings. For a moment, an owl was at my bedroom window. The last piece of the puzzle was in place, his spirit was free.

Shalom we called him. A prince of piece who touched in a special way everyone with whom he came in contact. He was a dog of Siberian Husky/German Shepherd mix and the owl called his name.

New Sailors of the Seas

Through the mist
    a mast is seen
  A ship ...
bringing new sailors of the sea.

Their songs and dances
are the sounds and movements
    which connect us
  through time and space.

Like dolphin and whale
    their kindred in the sea
Their play is their truth,
    their music, a message
      to be.

They are: forever windward bound
    forever crew
    forever family
in their journey through
      eternity.

New sailors of the seas.

Reflection

I do not seek another to feel complete
But,
To enjoy the reflection.

www.ingramcontent.com/pod-product-compliance
Lightning Source LLC
Chambersburg PA
CBHW071846290426
44109CB00017B/1946